# IB Economics

# Practice Questions with
# Answers

# for Numerical Question Paper 3

## George Graves

## About this book

Numerical questions will be a compulsory part of the higher level Economics exam under the new syllabus for first examination in May 2013. These questions will be examined in paper 3 and the requirement is to answer two out of three questions in one hour.

These questions aim to test the ability to make calculations through the application of basic mathematical principles consistent with higher level economic data. The level of mathematical ability required is within the scope of the standard level mathematics syllabus and knowledge of higher level mathematics is not necessary. Most calculations involve simple arithmetic, fractions and percentages.

This book provides a set of likely questions taken from parts of the higher level syllabus where calculations may be requested. The first part has a variety of short questions in order to familiarize the reader with the type of skills and techniques necessary. Detailed answers with explanations are also provided after each section.

The second part has two complete tests with detailed answers and explanations. Space is provided after each question for the reader to write the answer as will be the case with the actual exam paper. Each question is designed to be answered in 30 minutes.

Some of the questions are likely to be a bit more difficult than those in the final exam so successful completion of these questions should guarantee a good performance in the exam.

## Acknowledgements

I would like to thank my friend and colleague Evan Kladidis for patiently proof reading the text and providing invaluable guidance on how to present and set out numerical questions.

Many thanks also to my daughter Alkistis Elliott-Graves for corrections and help with the presentation of the text and diagrams.

Finally, a big thank you to Lydia, whose encouragement and support made the book possible.

## Author

George Graves has taught IB Economics in Greece since 1992 and regularly teaches OSC revision courses. He is currently an IB Higher Level examiner and is actively involved in setting up on-line revision courses for OSC.

## Dedication

I dedicate this book to Lydia and our children Alkistis and Leonie.

# Contents

# Part 1

**1. The weekly demand and supply functions for coffee in Atlantis are expressed by the following equations:**

$Qd = 90 - 10p$

$Qs = -30 + 30p$

Qd and Qs are the respective quantities in hundreds of sacks and p is the price per sack in €.

(a)  Calculate the equilibrium price and quantity.                    [2 marks]

..................................................................................................................
..................................................................................................................
..................................................................................................................
..................................................................................................................
..................................................................................................................
...............................................

(b) Fill in the Qd and Qs columns in the following table.                    [2 marks]

| Price (€ per sack) | Qd (00's sacks) | Qs (00's sacks) |
|---|---|---|
| 1 | | |
| 2 | | |
| 3 | | |
| 4 | | |
| 5 | | |

**If the government decided to provide a guaranteed price of €4 per sack of coffee and undertook to buy any quantity not sold in the market at the guaranteed price calculate:**

(c) The excess supply.                                                    [1 mark]

..................................................................................................................
..................................................................................................................

(d) The total cost to the government.                                    [2 marks]

..................................................................................................................
..................................................................................................................
..................................................................................................................

(e) The price elasticity of demand for this increase in price from €3 a sack to €4 a sack.

[2marks]

..................................................................................................................
..................................................................................................................
..................................................................................................................
..................................................................................................................

Assume an increase in the price of tea which causes the demand for coffee in Atlantis to increase by 40(00) sacks at all prices.

(f) State the equation for the new demand function.                      [2 marks]

..................................................................................................................
..................................................................................................................

(g) Find the new equilibrium price and quantity.                        [2 marks]

..................................................................................................................
..................................................................................................................

(h) Calculate the effect on the cost of the guaranteed price for the government.   [1 mark]

..................................................................................................................
..................................................................................................................

## 2. The following table shows the daily supply and demand functions for a good X.

| Qd | Price in $ | Qs |
|-----|-----|-----|
| 100 | 10 | 220 |
| 120 | 9 | 210 |
| 140 | 8 | 200 |
| 160 | 7 | 190 |
| 180 | 6 | 180 |
| 200 | 5 | 170 |
| 220 | 4 | 160 |
| 240 | 3 | 150 |
| 260 | 2 | 140 |

Assume that a specific tax of $3 per unit is imposed on good X

a) Calculate the new equilibrium price. [2 marks]

..........................................................................................................................................
..........................................................................................................................................

b) Calculate the total tax revenue to the government. [2 marks]

..........................................................................................................................................
..........................................................................................................................................

c) Calculate the total incidence of the tax on i) consumers and ii) producers. [2 marks]

..........................................................................................................................................
..........................................................................................................................................

If instead of a tax the government granted a subsidy of $3 per unit to the producers of X

d) Calculate the new equilibrium price and output. [2 marks]

..........................................................................................................................................
..........................................................................................................................................

e) Calculate the daily cost to the government of this subsidy. [2 marks]

..........................................................................................................................................
..........................................................................................................................................

3. The following table shows the daily output of workers producing handbags. Each handbag is sold for $20 and each worker is paid $100 a day.

| Workers | Handbags per day |
|---------|------------------|
| 0 | 0 |
| 1 | 10 |
| 2 | 25 |
| 3 | 45 |
| 4 | 60 |
| 5 | 72 |
| 6 | 80 |
| 7 | 85 |
| 8 | 82 |

a) Calculate the total wage cost of producing 60 handbags.                     [2 marks]

...................................................................................................................................
...................................................................................................................................
...................................................................................................................................

b) After the employment of how many workers do diminishing marginal returns set in?

[2 marks]

...................................................................................................................................
...................................................................................................................................

c) Calculate the marginal product of the 8$^{th}$ worker.                     [1 mark]

...................................................................................................................................
...................................................................................................................................

d) Calculate the value of handbags produced daily by the 6$^{th}$ worker.　　　　[2 marks]

...............................................................................................................................

...............................................................................................................................

If workers are the only variable factor and total fixed costs are $500 a day

e) Calculate the number of workers a profit maximizing producer would employ and the total profit.　　　　[5 marks]

...............................................................................................................................

...............................................................................................................................

...............................................................................................................................

...............................................................................................................................

...............................................................................................................................

If a 10% tax on profit was introduced

f) How would this affect the profit maximizing output?　　　　[1 mark]

...............................................................................................................................

...............................................................................................................................

g) Calculate the new level of profit.　　　　[2 marks]

...............................................................................................................................

...............................................................................................................................

...............................................................................................................................

**4. The following table shows the weekly total cost for a perfectly competitive corn farmer who can sell any amount of corn at the market price of $30 a bag**

| OUTPUT (Bags per Week) | TOTAL COST (TC) ($per bag) |
|---|---|
| 0 | 20 |
| 1 | 60 |
| 2 | 80 |
| 3 | 95 |
| 4 | 105 |
| 5 | 120 |
| 6 | 138 |
| 7 | 165 |
| 8 | 195 |
| 9 | 230 |
| 10 | 270 |

a) Calculate the average fixed cost for 4 units of output.                    [2 marks]

...................................................................................................................................
...................................................................................................................................

b) Calculate the average variable cost for 2 units of output.                    [2 marks]

...................................................................................................................................
...................................................................................................................................

c) Calculate the profit maximizing output.                    [4 marks]

...................................................................................................................................
...................................................................................................................................
...................................................................................................................................
...................................................................................................................................
...................................................................................................................................

d) Calculate the total profit. [2 marks]

.............................................................................................................................................

.............................................................................................................................................

e) Is the total profit calculated in d) normal profit or super normal (abnormal) profit?

[2 marks]

.............................................................................................................................................

.............................................................................................................................................

f) What would you expect to happen in this market in the long run and how would this affect this firm's price and output? [2 marks]

.............................................................................................................................................

.............................................................................................................................................

.............................................................................................................................................

g) Calculate the price that corresponds to the long run shut down point.

[2 marks]

.............................................................................................................................................

.............................................................................................................................................

.............................................................................................................................................

h) If market price increased to $35 calculate the new profit maximizing output and level of profit. [4 marks]

.............................................................................................................................................

.............................................................................................................................................

.............................................................................................................................................

.............................................................................................................................................

.............................................................................

**5. The following table relates to a section of the demand function faced by a monopolist.**

| Price ($ per unit) | Output (units per day) |
|---|---|
| 30 | 5 |
| 28 | 6 |
| 26 | 7 |
| 24 | 8 |
| 22 | 9 |
| 20 | 10 |
| 18 | 11 |
| 16 | 12 |
| 14 | 13 |
| 12 | 14 |
| 10 | 15 |

Assume that MC is constant at $10 per unit and FC is $100 a day.

a) Calculate the daily profit maximizing output and price.                [4 marks]

..................................................................................................
..................................................................................................
..................................................................................................
..................................................................................................
..................................................................................................
..................................................................................................

b) Calculate the total daily profit.                [2 marks]

..................................................................................................
..................................................................................................

c) At the monopolist's profit maximizing price is demand elastic or inelastic? Explain your answer.                [2 marks]

..................................................................................................
..................................................................................................

d) If the monopolist wanted to maximize revenue rather than profit, what price would be charged and what output would be produced? [2 marks]

..............................................................................................................................

..............................................................................................................................

e) If this monopolist was charging a price of $16 and selling 12 units per day what advice would you give in order to increase profit? [2 marks]

..............................................................................................................................

..............................................................................................................................

f) If the government forced the monopoly to operate at the point where allocative efficiency is achieved what price would the monopolist now set? [2 marks]

..............................................................................................................................

..............................................................................................................................

g) How would this allocatively efficient price affect profitability? [2 marks]

..............................................................................................................................

..............................................................................................................................

**If MC was zero**

h) What price would maximize profit? [2 marks]

..............................................................................................................................

..............................................................................................................................

i) Comment on the price elasticity of demand around this price? [2 marks]

..............................................................................................................................

..............................................................................................................................

**6. The following table shows the daily costs and revenue for a pie seller.**

| Quantity of Pies per day | Total Cost ($ per day) | Total Revenue ($ per day) |
|---|---|---|
| 0 | 4 | 0 |
| 10 | 6 | 10 |
| 20 | 9 | 19 |
| 30 | 13 | 27 |
| 40 | 18 | 34 |
| 50 | 24 | 40 |
| 60 | 31 | 45 |
| 70 | 39 | 49 |
| 80 | 48 | 51 |

a) Calculate the Total Variable Cost of producing 50 pies.                    [2 marks]

..................................................................................................................................

..................................................................................................................................

b) Calculate the profit maximizing output and price.                    [4 marks]

..................................................................................................................................

..................................................................................................................................

..................................................................................................................................

..................................................................................................................................

c) Is this firm operating in a perfectly competitive market? Explain your answer.

[3 marks]

..................................................................................................................................

..................................................................................................................................

..................................................................................................................................

d) At what price would 30 pies be sold? [2 marks]

...........................................................................................................................................

...........................................................................................................................................

**If Fixed Costs were to double:**

e) How would the profit maximizing price and quantity be affected? [2 marks]

...........................................................................................................................................

...........................................................................................................................................

f) Calculate the new level of profit. [2 marks]

...........................................................................................................................................

...........................................................................................................................................

g) Calculate Average Cost for producing 40 pies. [2 marks]

...........................................................................................................................................

...........................................................................................................................................

h) Calculate the percentage of Variable Costs to Total Cost when 50 pies are produced.

[2 marks]

...........................................................................................................................................

...........................................................................................................................................

...........................................................................................................................................

i) Calculate the Price Elasticity of Demand for the price change necessary to increase the quantity of pies sold from 50 to 60 per day. [4 marks]

...........................................................................................................................................

...........................................................................................................................................

...........................................................................................................................................

...........................................................................................................................................

...........................................................................................................................................

**7. The following table shows the weekly Marginal Revenue (MR) in $ for sales of the same product, by a monopolist, in 3 separate markets, A, B and C.**

| Units of Output | MR A | MR B | MR C |
|---|---|---|---|
| 1 | 24 | 14 | 12 |
| 2 | 20 | 12 | 10 |
| 3 | 16 | 10 | 8 |
| 4 | 12 | 8 | 6 |
| 5 | 8 | 6 | 4 |
| 6 | 4 | 4 | 2 |

Assuming that this monopolist produces 12 units per week and aims to maximize its profit:

a) Calculate how many units it will sell in each market per week.          [3 marks]

................................................................................................................................
................................................................................................................................
................................................................................................................................
................................................................................................................................

b) Calculate the price it would charge in each market.          [6 marks]

................................................................................................................................
................................................................................................................................
................................................................................................................................
................................................................................................................................
................................................................................................................................

**If Marginal Cost was constant at $4:**

c) How many units would it sell in each market and at what price?          [6 marks]

................................................................................................................................
................................................................................................................................
................................................................................................................................
................................................................................................................................
................................................................................................................................
................................................................................................................................
................................................................................................................................

**Assuming that each market has a linear demand function:**

d) Calculate the Marginal Revenue, Total Revenue and Average Revenue in each market for:

i) 7 units of output                                               [3 marks]

...................................................................................................

...................................................................................................

...................................................................................................

...................................................................................................

ii) 8 units of output                                              [3 marks]

...................................................................................................

...................................................................................................

...................................................................................................

...................................................................................................

e) Comment on the price elasticity of demand for the change in units from 7 to 8 in Market A

[2 marks]

...................................................................................................

...................................................................................................

...................................................................................................

f) At what price would the monopolist maximize Total Revenue in Market A?

[2 marks]

...................................................................................................

...................................................................................................

...................................................................................................

**8. The following information relates to the economy of Atlantis.**

| Annual Expenditure | $bn |
|---|---|
| Consumption (C) | 18 |
| Investment (I) | 5 |
| Government Spending (G) | 8 |
| Exports (X) | 3 |
| Imports (M) | 4 |

**Capital consumption = $2bn**

**Net Property Income from Abroad = -$1bn**

**MPC = 0.5**

**MPS = 0.2**

**MPT = 0.1**

**MPM = 0.2**

a) Calculate Gross Domestic Product. [2 marks]

...................................................................................................................

...................................................................................................................

b) Calculate Net National Product. [2 marks]

...................................................................................................................

...................................................................................................................

c) Calculate the total value of injections. [1 mark]

...................................................................................................................

d) Calculate the total value of withdrawals necessary for Income to be in equilibrium.

[1 mark]

...................................................................................................................

e) Calculate the external deficit as a % of GDP. [2 marks]

...................................................................................................................

...................................................................................................................

**If the Government increases it spending to $10bn as a result of a road building programme:**

f) Calculate the value of the multiplier. [2 marks]

......................................................................................................................................
......................................................................................................................................
......................................................................................................................................

g) Calculate the new equilibrium level of Income. [2 marks]

......................................................................................................................................
......................................................................................................................................

h) Calculate the new value of imports. [2 marks]

......................................................................................................................................
......................................................................................................................................

i) Calculate the new value of consumption. [2 marks]

......................................................................................................................................
......................................................................................................................................

**9.** The following table gives the value (in $millions) of Income (Y), Consumption (C), Savings (S) and Investment (I) for a closed economy with no government sector.

| Y | C | S | I |
|------|-----|---|----|
| 0 | 200 | | 40 |
| 100 | 260 | | 40 |
| 200 | 320 | | 40 |
| 300 | 380 | | 40 |
| 400 | 440 | | 40 |
| 500 | 500 | | 40 |
| 600 | 560 | | 40 |
| 700 | 620 | | 40 |
| 800 | 680 | | 40 |
| 900 | 740 | | 40 |
| 1000 | 800 | | 40 |

a) Fill in the S column. [2 marks]

b) Calculate the value of MPC and MPS. [2 marks]

..................................................................................................................
..................................................................................................................

c) Find the equilibrium level of income. [2 marks]

..................................................................................................................
..................................................................................................................

d) At what level of income is the Average Propensity to Consume (APC) = 1? [2 marks]

..................................................................................................................
..................................................................................................................

**If I increased to 80 at each level of Y.**

e) Calculate the new equilibrium level of income. [2 marks]

..................................................................................................................
..................................................................................................................

f) If full employment (YF) is at Y = 900 calculate the size of the deflationary gap

[2 marks]

.............................................................................................................................

.............................................................................................................................

g) Calculate the value of the multiplier.                                    [2 marks]

.............................................................................................................................

.............................................................................................................................

h) Calculate the increase in I necessary to close the deflationary gap.        [2 marks]

.............................................................................................................................

.............................................................................................................................

.............................................................................................................................

**10.** The following table shows the rate of tax applied to different levels of income for wage earners in Atlantis. Value Added Tax (VAT) is imposed on all expenditure at a rate of 18%.

| Annual Income ($) | Tax rate (%) |
|---|---|
| 0- 4000 | 0 |
| 4001-10000 | 20 |
| 10001-20000 | 25 |
| 20001- 40000 | 30 |
| 40001 + | 50 |

- **Bill earns $4000 and spends 50% of his disposable income**
- **Bob earns $30000 and spends 60% of his disposable income**
- **Mary earns $80000 and spends 75% of her disposable income**

a) Calculate the total tax paid by Bill, Bob and Mary.                    [9 marks]

Bill:................................................................................................................

................................................................................................................

................................................................................................................

Bob:................................................................................................................

................................................................................................................

................................................................................................................

Mary:................................................................................................................

................................................................................................................

................................................................................................................

b) Calculate the % of income paid in tax for each worker.                    [3 marks]

................................................................................................................

................................................................................................................

................................................................................................................

................................................................................................................

................................................................................................................

................................................................................................................

................................................................................................................

c) With respect to the tax on earnings, calculate the average and marginal tax rates for Bill, Bob and Mary. [3 marks]

Bill:..............................................................................................................................

................................................................................................................................

................................................................................................................................

Bob:..............................................................................................................................

................................................................................................................................

................................................................................................................................

Mary:..............................................................................................................................

................................................................................................................................

................................................................................................................................

d) From your answer to c) above, would you describe the tax on income in Atlantis to be progressive or regressive? Explain your answer. [3 marks]

................................................................................................................................

................................................................................................................................

................................................................................................................................

**If the tax system now changes so that everyone pays 25% tax on all earnings and VAT is raised to 20%:**

e) Calculate the total tax paid by Bill, Bob and Mary. [6 marks]

Bill:

................................................................................................................................

................................................................................................................................

Bob:

................................................................................................................................

................................................................................................................................

Mary:

................................................................................................................................

................................................................................................................................

f) Calculate the % of earnings paid in tax by Bill, Bob and Mary. [3 marks]

Bill:

...........................................................................................................................

...........................................................................................................................

Bob:

...........................................................................................................................

...........................................................................................................................

Mary:

...........................................................................................................................

...........................................................................................................................

g) Has the tax system become more or less progressive? Explain your answer. [2 marks]

...........................................................................................................................

...........................................................................................................................

h) Will the Gini coefficient for Atlantis be larger or smaller than before? [2 marks]

...........................................................................................................................

...........................................................................................................................

**11.** The following table shows the prices and weights of a representative sample of products used to calculate a consumer price index (CPI).

| Product | Price in 2000 ($) | Price in 2001 ($) | Weight/100 |
|---|---|---|---|
| A | 2.00 | 2.10 | 20 |
| B | 1.50 | 1.60 | 25 |
| C | 0.80 | 0.75 | 10 |
| D | 1.00 | 1.05 | 30 |
| E | 0.40 | 0.45 | 15 |

**Assuming that 2000 is the base year so that the CPI is 100 in 2000:**

a) Calculate a weighted price index for 2001.                    [4marks]

........................................................................................................................
........................................................................................................................
........................................................................................................................
........................................................................................................................
........................................................................................................................
........................................................................................................................
........................................................................................................................

b) Calculate the average % increase in prices from 2000 to 2001.          [2 marks]

........................................................................................................................
........................................................................................................................

c) Explain the difference in your answers to a) and b).               [2 marks]

........................................................................................................................
........................................................................................................................

d) If Sara spent $200 on this sample of products in 2000 how much would she spend to buy the same sample of products in 2001?                    [1 mark]

........................................................................................................................

**If John spends all his income on product C**

e) Calculate the % change in his real income between 2000 and 2001.                    [3 marks]

..................................................................................................................

..................................................................................................................

..................................................................................................................

f) If John's real income in 2000 was represented by the index number 100, calculate the index number (to the nearest whole number) that would represent his real income in 2001.

[2 marks]

..................................................................................................................

..................................................................................................................

..................................................................................................................

g) What does your answer to f) suggest about the accuracy of index numbers as a measure of the cost of living?                    [2 marks]

..................................................................................................................

..................................................................................................................

**12. The CPI for Atlantis is shown in the following table:**

| Year | 1998 | 1999 | 2000 | 2001 | 2002 | 2003 | 2004 | 2005 |
|------|------|------|------|------|------|------|------|------|
| CPI | 96 | 100 | 102 | 105 | 104 | 103 | 103 | 102 |

a) Which year is the base year?                                      [1 mark]

.................................................................................................................

b) In which year did Atlantis face the highest rate of inflation?    [2 marks]

.................................................................................................................

.................................................................................................................

c) Calculate the % rate of inflation for that year.                  [2 marks]

.................................................................................................................

.................................................................................................................

d) Calculate the rate of inflation for 2001.                         [2 marks]

.................................................................................................................

.................................................................................................................

e) In 2005 were prices higher than in 1998? Explain your answer.     [2 marks]

.................................................................................................................

.................................................................................................................

f) In 2005 were prices higher than in 2001? Explain your answer.     [2 marks]

.................................................................................................................

.................................................................................................................

g) From 2001 to 2005 is Atlantis suffering from inflation, deflation or disinflation? Explain your answer.                                                    [2 marks]

.................................................................................................................

.................................................................................................................

**13. The following figures relate to the economy of Boozyland which only produces wine, beer and cheese.**

| Product | Output 2000 | Output 2005 | Price 2000 ($ per unit) | Price 2005 ($ per unit) |
|---------|-------------|-------------|--------------------------|--------------------------|
| Wine | 100 | 200 | 2 | 3 |
| Beer | 100 | 250 | 3 | 4 |
| Cheese | 100 | 140 | 1 | 1.5 |

a) Calculate nominal GDP in Boozyland in 2000 and in 2005.                [2 marks]

...........................................................................................................................
...........................................................................................................................
...........................................................................................................................

b) Calculate the % increase in nominal GDP from 2000 to 2005.                [1 mark]

...........................................................................................................................
...........................................................................................................................

c) Calculate the real GDP in 2005 at 2000 prices.                [4 marks]

...........................................................................................................................
...........................................................................................................................
...........................................................................................................................
...........................................................................................................................

d) Calculate the % increase in real GDP from 2000 to 2005.                [2 marks]

...........................................................................................................................
...........................................................................................................................

**14. The following table shows employment figures in millions (m) for Atlantis.**

| Year | Population of Working Age (m) | Labour Force (m) | Total Employment (m) |
|------|------------------------------|------------------|----------------------|
| 2004 | 20.5 | 11.5 | 10.2 |
| 2005 | 21 | 11.8 | 10.6 |
| 2006 | 21.2 | 12.2 | 11.1 |
| 2007 | 21.5 | 12.5 | 11.2 |
| 2008 | 22 | 12.8 | 10.8 |

a) Calculate the number of workers unemployed in 2006 and 2008.                    [2 marks]

...................................................................................................................

...................................................................................................................

b) Calculate the rate of unemployment as a % for all the years.                    [4 marks]

...................................................................................................................

...................................................................................................................

...................................................................................................................

...................................................................................................................

c) If in 2008 there were 200000 job vacancies, what would be the most likely type of unemployment in Atlantis? Explain your answer.                    [4 marks]

...................................................................................................................

...................................................................................................................

...................................................................................................................

...................................................................................................................

15. The following table refers to the Exchange Rate and relative prices for country A whose currency is the $ and country B whose currency is the €.

| Year | Exchange Rate $/€ | Price Index in A (2003 = 100) | Price index in B (2003 = 100) |
|------|-------------------|-------------------------------|-------------------------------|
| 2000 | 1.80 | 98 | 94 |
| 2006 | 1.62 | 102 | 106 |

a) Which country's currency has depreciated between 2000 and 2006?          [1 mark]

................................................................................................................................

b) Calculate the currency depreciation as a %.          [2 marks]

................................................................................................................................
................................................................................................................................

c) Calculate the real exchange rate for country B in 2000 and 2006.          [4 marks]

................................................................................................................................
................................................................................................................................
................................................................................................................................
................................................................................................................................

d) Calculate the purchasing power parity exchange rate (PPP) in 2006.          [4 marks]

................................................................................................................................
................................................................................................................................
................................................................................................................................
................................................................................................................................
................................................................................................................................

e) Assuming trade takes place between A and B at the PPP exchange rate calculated in d), and there are no transport costs, calculate the $ price in A of a good imported from B which sells for €10 in B.          [3 marks]

................................................................................................................................
................................................................................................................................
................................................................................................................................

**16.** The following table shows the world price of coffee and the production of coffee by Atlantis. Coffee is the only export of Atlantis and it exports all of its coffee production.

| Year | Price of Coffee ($ per bag) | Index of Coffee Price | Coffee Production and Export (million bags) | Index of coffee Production | Index of Import Prices |
|------|------|------|------|------|------|
| 2001 | 11 | | 6 | | 90 |
| 2002 | 12 | | 6.5 | | 95 |
| 2003 | 14 | 100 | 7.2 | 100 | 100 |
| 2004 | 13 | | 7.5 | | 106 |
| 2005 | 18 | | 6.2 | | 110 |
| 2006 | 19 | | 6.8 | | 112 |
| 2007 | 22 | | 7.3 | | 110 |

a) Fill in the columns for Index of coffee price and index of coffee production using 2003 as the base year. [6 marks]

b) Calculate the value of Atlantis' exports in 2001 and 2007. [2 marks]

....................................................................................................................................

....................................................................................................................................

c) Calculate the Terms of Trade for Atlantis. [4 marks]

....................................................................................................................................

....................................................................................................................................

....................................................................................................................................

....................................................................................................................................

d) Describe the movement of the Terms of Trade from 2001 to 2007. [2 marks]

....................................................................................................................................

....................................................................................................................................

....................................................................................................................................

e)  If the total spending on imports in 2001 was $72m, calculate net exports.     [2 marks]

..........................................................................................................................
..........................................................................................................................
..........................................................................................................................

f) If the balance of net exports calculated in e) is 3% of GDP, calculate GDP for Atlantis.

[2 marks]

..........................................................................................................................
..........................................................................................................................
..........................................................................................................................

**17. The following diagram shows the effect on the imports of steel of the imposition of a tariff of $20 a tonne on imported steel.**

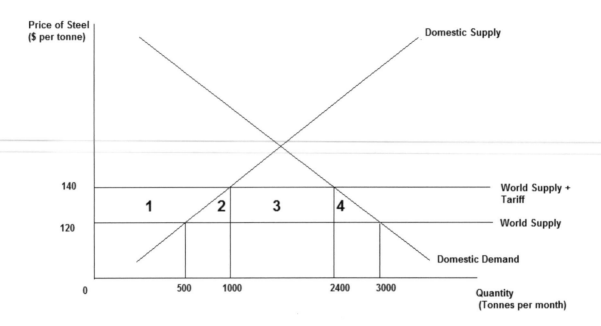

a) Calculate the revenue per month, received by the government, from this tariff.   [2 marks]

...................................................................................................................................

...................................................................................................................................

b) Calculate the reduction in the volume of imports per month.                    [1 mark]

...................................................................................................................................

...................................................................................................................................

c) Calculate the monthly loss of export revenues to world steel producers as a result of the tariff. [2 marks]

.........................................................................................................................
.........................................................................................................................
.........................................................................................................................

d) Calculate the total loss of consumer surplus to consumers each month. [4 marks]

.........................................................................................................................
.........................................................................................................................
.........................................................................................................................
.........................................................................................................................
.........................................................................................................................

e) Calculate the total monthly deadweight loss as a result of the tariff. [2 marks]

.........................................................................................................................
.........................................................................................................................
.........................................................................................................................

f) Calculate the monthly % change in the total expenditure on steel as a result of the tariff on steel. [3 marks]

.........................................................................................................................
.........................................................................................................................
.........................................................................................................................
.........................................................................................................................

g) If a car producer uses 500 tonnes of steel per month calculate the increase in its monthly costs of production as a result of the tariff. [2 marks]

.........................................................................................................................
.........................................................................................................................
.........................................................................................................................

**18. The following data refers to the production possibilities of two countries A and B, for the production of wine and cars.**

**Country A can produce either 20 cars and 0 wine or 0 cars and 100 wine and has a constant opportunity cost ratio of 1 car: 5 wine.**

**Country B can produce either 10 cars and 0 wine or 0 cars and 200 wine and has a constant opportunity cost ratio of 1 car: 20 wine.**

a) Which country has an Absolute Advantage (AA) in Cars and which has an Absolute Advantage in wine?                                                              [2 marks]

..................................................................................................................................................
..................................................................................................................................................
..................................................................................................................................................

b) Which country has a Comparative Advantage (CA) in Cars and which has a Comparative Advantage in wine?                                                              [2 marks]

..................................................................................................................................................
..................................................................................................................................................
..................................................................................................................................................

c) How do your answers to a) and b) help to determine whether countries A and B should trade with each other?                                                              [4 marks]

..................................................................................................................................................
..................................................................................................................................................
..................................................................................................................................................
..................................................................................................................................................

d) Calculate the total number of cars and wine that would be produced if country A and B specialized completely in accordance with the principle of comparative advantage.

[2 marks]

..................................................................................................................................................
..................................................................................................................................................
..................................................................................................................................................

e) If countries A and B wanted to be self-sufficient in both cars and wine and devoted half of their resources to car production and half to wine production, calculate the total production of cars and wine.                                                              [2 marks]

..................................................................................................................................................
..................................................................................................................................................
..................................................................................................................................................

f) On the grid below draw and label the appropriate axes and draw the graphs illustrating the production possibility functions for country A and B.                    [4 marks]

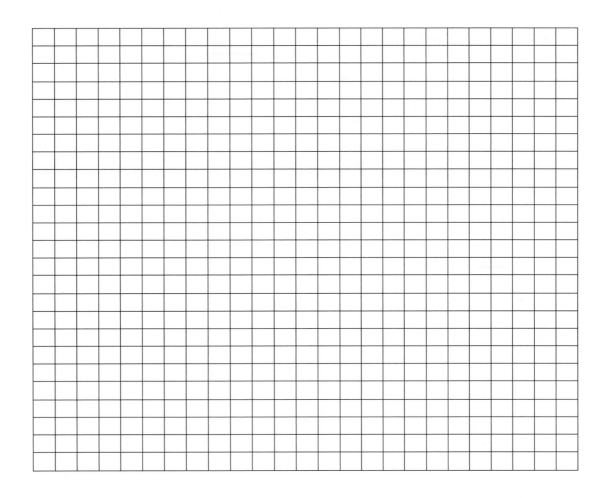

g) At an exchange rate of 1 car for 10 wines and assuming no additional costs, calculate what country A would gain by exporting 2 cars to country B and what country B would gain by importing 2 cars from country A.                    [4 marks]

.......................................................................................................................................
.......................................................................................................................................
.......................................................................................................................................
.......................................................................................................................................
.......................................................................................................................................

## Question 1

a) We know that in equilibrium Qd = Qs so

$$90 - 10p = -30 + 30p$$

$$90 + 30 = 10p + 30p$$

$$120 = 40p$$

$$p = 120/40 = €3 \qquad\qquad \text{(1 mark)}$$

Having found the price we now substitute it in either the Qd or Qs equation.

e.g.   Qd = 90 – (10x3)

= 90 – 30

= 60(00's) sacks = 6000 sacks per week.          (1 mark)

(b)

| Price (€ per sack) | Qd (00's sacks) | Qs (00's sacks) |
|:---:|:---:|:---:|
| 1 | 80 | 0 |
| 2 | 70 | 30 |
| 3 | 60 | 60 |
| 4 | 50 | 90 |
| 5 | 40 | 120 |

(2 marks)

We have already found the equilibrium price of € 3 and equilibrium quantity of 60 and we use the same method of substituting each price into the functions to find the other quantities.

E.g. at price 2, Qd = 90 – (10 x 2) = 90 – 20 = 70

and   Qs = – 30 + ( 30 x 2 ) = – 30 + 60 = 30

Since the supply and demand functions are linear it not necessary to make all the calculations. It is clear that for every unit price change, demand changes by 10 and supply changes by 30.

This can also be applied to questions that ask you to plot the demand and/or supply functions on a graph. Two points are sufficient to draw the straight line (linear) functions.

*Question 1 Continued*

c) From the table it is clear that at a price of €4, Qd = 50(00) and Qs = 90(00) so the excess supply is 90(00) – 50(00) = 4000

d) The total cost to the government will be

$$40(00) \times €4 = €16000$$

e) The price elasticity of demand is calculated as

% change in Qd/ % change in price = (-) 16.6/ 33.3

$$= (-) 0.5$$

f) Since Qd has increased by 40(00) sacks at all prices the new equation will be

$$Qd = (90+40) - 10p$$

$$= 130 - 10p$$

g) Equilibrium price is where Qd = Qs so

$$130 - 10p = -30 + 30p$$
$$130 + 30 = 30p + 10p$$
$$160 = 40p$$
$$P = 160/40 = 40$$

h) The cost to the government is now zero because the new equilibrium price is equal to the guaranteed price and there is no longer any excess supply.

a) A specific tax will shift the supply function parallel to the left by the vertical distance corresponding to the tax i.e. $3. Since the supply function is presented in the table as quantities per price we have to find the new supply at each price. To do this we move the supply figures up by 3 places corresponding to the $3 tax. What used to be supplied at $2 will now be supplied at $5. What used to be supplied at $3 will now be supplied at $6 and so on. The new price will be $7 where the new supply equals the demand at 160 units.

b) The tax revenue received by the government is: (tax per unit) x (the new equilibrium quantity) = $3 x 160 = $480

c) i) The incidence on consumers is:  (the price increase) x 160 = $1 x 160 = $160

ii) The incidence on producers is:  (the remainder of the tax) x 160 = $2 x 160 = $320.

d) In the case of a subsidy the effect is the exact opposite of the tax i.e. the supply figures move down by 3 places so the new equilibrium price is $5 and quantity is 200

e) The cost to the government will be:

(the subsidy) x (the new equilibrium quantity) = $3 x 200 = $600

**Some tips**

Do not make the mistake of putting all the tax on the price. The incidence of a tax will always be shared between consumers (who pay the price increase) and producers (who pay the rest), assuming normal supply and demand functions. Only in the case of perfectly inelastic demand or perfectly elastic supply would all of the tax go on the price and therefore on the consumer.

## Question 3

a) To produce 60 handbags requires 4 workers so the total wage cost is 4 x $100 = $400

b) To find where diminishing returns occur we have to calculate the marginal product (MP) for each additional worker. We find that the MP for the 3$^{rd}$ worker is 20 and for the 4$^{th}$ worker is 15 so diminishing returns occur with the employment of the 4$^{th}$ worker

c) The marginal product of the 8$^{th}$ worker is – 3 since this is the change in total product (TP) brought about by employing the 8$^{th}$ worker.

TP for 7 workers = 85 and TP for 8 workers = 82.

d) The 6$^{th}$ worker produces an additional 8 handbags which sell for $20 so the value is

8 x $20 = $160

e) A profit maximizing producer would employ workers up to the point where the value of MP is equal to the wage.

To find the value of MP we multiply MP by $20.

The 7$^{th}$ worker has MP = 5 and so value of MP = 5 x $20 = $100.

The wage is $100 so 7 workers will be employed.

The total profit will be equal to the total revenue minus the total cost.

The total revenue = number of handbags x $20 = 85 x $20 = $1700.

The total cost = fixed cost + variable cost = $500 + (7 x $100) = $1200.

Total profit = $1700 – $1200 = $500.

f) A tax on profit would have no effect on the profit maximizing output because it does not affect the value of marginal product or marginal cost.

g) The new level of profit will be $500 – 10% = $500 – $50 = $450.

## Question 4

a) Average Fixed Cost (AFC) = Total Fixed Cost (TFC)/Output

TFC is equal to the total cost at zero output = $20

$$\text{So AFC} = \$20/4 = \$5.$$

b) Average Variable Cost (AVC) = Total Variable Cost (TVC)/Output

TVC = TC – TFC = $80 - $20 = $60

AVC = $60/2 = $30.

c) The profit maximizing output can be found by two methods.

Method 1: Find the output where marginal revenue (MR) = marginal cost (MC)

MR = $30. We know this because the corn farmer is in a perfectly competitive market so

MR = price = $30

MC needs to be calculated by the change in TC for each unit of output as shown in the following table:

| Output | TC | MC |
|--------|-----|-----|
| 0 | 20 | - |
| 1 | 60 | 40 |
| 2 | 80 | 20 |
| 3 | 95 | 15 |
| 4 | 105 | 10 |
| 5 | 120 | 15 |
| 6 | 138 | 18 |
| 7 | 165 | 27 |
| 8 | 195 | 30 |
| 9 | 230 | 35 |
| 10 | 270 | 40 |

From the table above we see that MC = $30 for 8 units of output so this will be the profit maximizing output.

**Method 2**: As an alternative we can calculate the total revenue (TR) for each output (units of output x $30) and subtract the TC from this. The largest output with the highest profit will be the profit maximizing output.

d) Total profit = TR – TC

At output 8, TR = 8 x $30 = $240, TC = $195 so total profit = $45.

e) Since TR is greater than TC it is supernormal profit.

f) In the long run new firms will enter this market attracted by the super normal profit and as a result the market price will fall and each firm will produce less than before.

g) The long run shut down point is the price for which only normal profit will be earned which is the lowest point of Average Cost. The lowest Average Cost is $23 and this is the lowest price at which a firm could remain in production in the long run.

h) If the market price increased to $35 the profit maximizing output would increase to 9 units where MC = MR = $35 and the new level of profit would be $85.

Question 5

Profit is maximized where MC = MR, we know that MC = $10 so we need to calculate MR. For this we need to calculate TR and it would be sensible to construct a new table with TC, TR and MR as follows:

| Price, P ($per unit) | Output, Q (units per day) | TR | MR | TC |
| --- | --- | --- | --- | --- |
| 30 | 5 | 150 | | 150 |
| 28 | 6 | 168 | 18 | 160 |
| 26 | 7 | 182 | 14 | 170 |
| 24 | 8 | 192 | 10 | 180 |
| 22 | 9 | 198 | 6 | 190 |
| 20 | 10 | 200 | 2 | 200 |
| 18 | 11 | 198 | -2 | 210 |
| 16 | 12 | 192 | -6 | 220 |
| 14 | 13 | 182 | -10 | 230 |
| 12 | 14 | 168 | -14 | 240 |
| 10 | 15 | 150 | -18 | 250 |

TR = P x Q, MR = Change in TR brought about from sale of an additional unit,

TC = Q x MC +$100 Fixed cost.

From the table we see that MR = MC = $10 at an output of 8 and a price of $24.

b) Total profit = TR –TC = $192– $180 = $12

c) Demand is elastic (MR is +)

d) The revenue maximizing price is $20 where TR = $200 and Q = 10.

e) An increase in price would lead to an increase in profit because demand is inelastic at this price.

f) Allocative efficiency is achieved when production is where P = MC = $10.

g) At this price TR = $150 and TC = $250 so there would be a loss of $100.

h) If MC = 0 then profit will be maximized where total revenue is maximized at price $20.

i) Around this price of $20, where TR is Maximised, demand is of unit elasticity.

## Question 6

a) TVC = TC – TFC. From the table we see that TC for 50 pies = $24, and since TC for 0 output = $4 this corresponds to the TFC. TVC = $24 – $4 = $20

b) Profit maximization can be found either by equating MC and MR or simply subtracting TC from TR. MC = MR = $6 for 50 pies and price = AR = TR/Q = $40/50 = $0.80.

c) This firm is not operating in perfect competition because it faces a downward sloping demand and not a perfectly elastic demand.

d) Price = AR so for 30 pies AR = TR/Q = $27/30 = $0.90.

e) If FC double this will not affect profit maximization because MC and MR are unaffected.

f) The new level of profit will be $4 less than previously because FC is now $8 per day. Total profit was $40 – $24 = $16, new profit = $16 – $4 = $12.

g) AC = TC/Q = $22/40 = $0.55.

h) For 50 pies TC = $28, FC = $8 so VC = $28 – $8 = $20.

Required % = 20/28 x 100 = 71.43%

i) The price change necessary for an increase in sales from 50 to 60 is from $0.80 to $0.75.

PED = % ΔQD/% ΔP = 20%/6.25% = 3.1 = elastic.

## Question 7

a) To find the profit maximizing output for 12 units between the 3 markets, we equate the MR in each market, thus 5 units in market A, 4 units in market B and 3 units in market C. Total units = 12, MR in each market = $8.

b) To calculate the price in each market we first calculate the TR by adding the MR for each additional unit and divide each TR by Q to find AR. E.g. in market A, MR for Q1 = $24, MR for Q2 = $20 so TR for Q2 = $24 + $20 = $44. AR = $44/2 = $22 and so on.

TR for 5 units in market A = $80, AR = $80/5 = $16

TR for 4 units in market B = $44, AR = $44/4 = $11

TR for 3 units in market C = $30, AR = $30/3 = $10.

c) With constant MC = $4, we equate with MR = $4 in each market, so 6 units in market A, at price $84/6 = $14, 6 units in market B, at price $54/6 = $9 and 5 units in market C, at price $40/5 = $8.

d) Assuming linear demand functions means that AR and MR are straight lines so MR will continue to fall by the same rate in each market i.e. by 4 per unit in market A, by 2 per unit in market B, and by 2 per unit in market C. AR and TR are calculated as for part b)

i) For 7 units MR in A = 0, MR in B = 2 and MR in C = 0.

ii) For 8 units MR in A = -4, MR in B = 0 and MR in C = -2.

e) For the change 7 to 8 in market A, MR is negative so it means that demand must be inelastic.

f) TR is maximized where MR = 0 which is at 7 units in market A so price = (TR/Q)

$$= \$84/7 = \$12$$

## Question 8

a) GDP = Total Spending = C + I + G + (X- M) = $18bn +$5bn + $8bn + ($3-$4) = $30bn

b) NNP = GDP – capital consumption (for Net) + net property income from abroad (for National). So NNP = $30bn – $2bn + (– $1bn) = $27bn.

c) Injections = I + G + X = $5bn + $8bn + $3bn = $16bn

d) In equilibrium Injections = Withdrawals = $16bn

e) (X-M) as % of GDP is $1bn as % of $30bn = 3.33%

f) An increase in G to $10bn is an increase of $2bn.

The multiplier = 1/(1-MPC) = 1/MPW = 1/0.5 = 2.

g) The new equilibrium income will be the original + the change through the multiplier.

  = $30bn + ($2bn x 2) = $34.

h) New value of imports = original ($4bn) + 0.2 x change in income

    = $4bn + (0.2 x $4bn) = $4.8bn

i) New value of Consumption = original ($18bn) + 0.5 x change in income

    =$18 + (0.5 x $4bn) = $20bn.

---

## Question 9

a) To fill in the S column apply the equation S = Y – C, since Y = C+S

| Y | C | S | I |
|------|-----|------|----|
| 0 | 200 | -200 | 40 |
| 100 | 260 | -160 | 40 |
| 200 | 320 | -120 | 40 |
| 300 | 380 | -80 | 40 |
| 400 | 440 | -40 | 40 |
| 500 | 500 | 0 | 40 |
| 600 | 560 | 40 | 40 |
| 700 | 620 | 80 | 40 |
| 800 | 680 | 120 | 40 |
| 900 | 740 | 160 | 40 |
| 1000 | 800 | 200 | 40 |

b) MPC = $\Delta C/\Delta Y$ = 60/100 = 0.6.  MPS = 1- MPC = 0.4

c) Equilibrium income is established where Y = C + I. This occurs at Y = 600

d) APC = C/Y. For APC to = 1 requires that C = Y = 500

e) If I increases to 80 new equilibrium income will be where (C + I) = Y.

        This occurs at Y = 700

f) If full employment is at Y = 900 the deflationary gap = Y – (C+I) = 900 – (740 + 80)

    = 80

g) The value of the multiplier (K) is 1/MPS = 1/0.4 = 2.5

h) The change in I needed to close the gap is $\Delta Y/K$ = 80/ 2.5 = 32.


## Question 10

a)

    i) Bill pays no income tax so his disposable income (Yd) = $4000. He spends 50% so indirect tax = 18% of 50% of Yd = 18% of $2000 = $360.

    ii) Bob's income tax = 20% of $6000 + 25% of $10000 + 30% of $10000

        = $1200 + $2500 + $3000 = $6700.

    Bob's Yd = $30000 – $6700 = $23300. He spends 60% Yd = $13980 and pays 18% tax on this = $2516.4.

    Bob's total tax = $6700 + $2516.4 = $9216.4.

    iii) Mary's income tax = 20% of $6000 + 25% of $10000 + 30% of $20000 + 50% of $40000

    = $1200 + $2500 + $6000 + $20000 = $29700.

    Mary's Yd = $80000 – $29700 = $50300. She spends 75% Yd = $37725 and pays 18% tax on this = $6790.5.

    Mary's total tax = $29700 + $6790.5 = $36490.5.

b) To express total tax paid as % of income we apply the following method:

(Total tax/income) x 100.

Using our results from a) we have:

Bill = ($360/$4000) x 100 = 9%

Bob = ($9216.4/$30000) x 100 = 30.7%

Mary = ($36490.5/$80000) x 100 = 45.6%


c) Average tax rate (ATR) = (total income tax/ income) x 100

Marginal tax rate (MTR) = highest rate of income tax paid on income.

For Bill both ATR and MTR are 0 because he pays no income tax.

For Bob ATR = ($6700/$30000) x 100 = 22.33% and MTR = 30%

For Mary ATR = ($29700/$80000) x 100 = 37.1% and MTR = 50%

d) The tax system is progressive because the ATR<MTR and ATR increases with income.

e) With the tax changes Bill now pays income tax of $1000 and Indirect tax of 20% on 50% of Yd. Yd = $3000 and spending = 50% = $1500 so VAT = 20% of $1500 = $300.

Bill's Total Tax = $1000 + $300 = $1300.

Using the same method we calculate Bob's Total Tax as $7500 + $2700 = $10200

And Mary's Total Tax as $20000 + $9000 = $29000.

f) As a % of income these Total Tax payments are:

Bill = ($1300/$4000) x 100 = 32.5%

Bob = ($10200/$30000) x 100 = 34%

Mary = ($29000/$80000) x 100 =36.25%

g) The tax system has become less progressive because the ATR>MTR and has increased for the lowest earner and has decreased for the highest earner.

h) Since income tax has stopped being progressive and the tax system has become more regressive, there will be a redistribution of income in favour of higher income groups so the Gini coefficient will increase as the Lorenz curve for Atlantis moves away from the 45 degree line.

## Question 11

a) To calculate a weighted index we have to make the following calculations:

(1) Price x Weight in base year

(2) Price x Weight in 2001

[Sum of (2)/Sum of (1)] x 100 = (127.75/121.5) x 100 =105.1

b) To find the % change in price we add the prices in base year and add the prices in 2001 and divide the difference with the sum for 2000 x 100.

P for 2000 = 5.7

P for 2001 = 5.95

% Difference = (0.25/5.7 x 100) = 4.38%

c) The % change is less than the weighted change because some items which are more widely bought have increased in price by more than the average

d) Sara will now spend $200 x (105.1/100) = $210.2

e) John's real income will increase by 6.25% as this is the % decrease in the price of product C.

f) The index of John's real income for 2001 would be 106 indicating the 6.25% increase.

g) A CPI is not a fully accurate measure of the cost of living, because different consumer groups have different spending habits, e.g. young people buy different products than old people.

## Question 12

a) The base year is 1999 because CPI = 100

b) The highest inflation is in 1999

c) % inflation = (100/96) x 100 = 104.16, therefore % inflation = 4.2%

d) Inflation for 2001 = (105/102) x 100 = 102.9 therefore % inflation = 2.9%

e) Yes, because CPI index has increased from 96 to 105

f) No, because CPI index has decreased from 105 to 102

g) Deflation, because CPI index has fallen indicating that prices have fallen

## Question 13

a) To calculate nominal GDP we calculate the value of output in each year = Output x Price

So for 2000: Wine = $200, Beer = $300 and Cheese = $100 Total = $600.

For 2005: Wine = $600, Beer = $1000 and Cheese = $210 Total = $1810

b) % increase in nominal GDP = [($1810 – $600)/$600] x 100 = 201.6%

c) To find real GDP for 2005 at 2000 prices we multiply 2005 output by 2000 prices

So: Wine = $400, Beer = $750 and Cheese = $140. Real GDP for 2005 = $1290

d) % increase in real GDP = [($1290 – $600)/$600] x 100 = 115

## Question 14

a) We find the number unemployed by subtracting the number employed from the Labour Force. So for 2006 = 12.2m – 11.1m = 1.1m and for 2008 = 12.8m-10.8m = 2m

b) To calculate the rate of unemployment we divide the number unemployed by the Labour Force and multiply this number by 100to give a %.

For 2004: [(11.5m – 10.2m)/11.5m] x 100 = 11.3%. Using the same method we find

For 2005: 10.2%, for 2006: 9%, for 2007: 10.4% and for 2008: 15.6%.

c) In 2008 there are 2m unemployed and 200000 job vacancies. This means that the total of frictional and structural unemployment is around 200 000 so even if all vacancies were filled there would still be 1.8m unemployed. It is therefore most likely that the majority suffer from Demand Deficient or Cyclical unemployment.

## Question 15

a) The € has depreciated from $1.80 to $1.62

b) The % depreciation is [($1.80 – $1.62)/$1.80] x 100 = 10%

c) The real exchange rate is calculated as: (€ Price/$ Price) x $/€ exchange rate

For 2000: (94/98) x 1.80 = 1.73

For 2006: (106/102) x 1.62 = 1.68

d) The PPP exchange rate is found by dividing the $ price increase in country A by the € price increase in country B and multiplying by the 2000 exchange rate.

Price increase in A = 102/98 = 1.040

Price increase in B = 106/94 = 1.127

So PPP exchange rate = (1.040/1.127) x 1.80 = 1.66

e) At the PPP exchange rate a product that costs €10 in country B would sell for:

10 x 1.66 = $16.6

## Question 16

a) To fill in the columns we have to calculate the coffee price index and the coffee production index.

To calculate the index for each year we take the price in that year, divide it by the base year price and multiply by 100.

e.g. For 2004 the coffee price index is: (13/14) x 100 = 92.8

For 2005 the index is: (18/14) x 100 = 128.6 and so on.

The index of coffee production is similarly calculated as: production in one year divided by production in base year x 100.

e.g. For 2004 the coffee production index is: (7.5/7.2) x 100 = 104.2 and so on.

| Year | Price of Coffee ($ per bag) | Index of Coffee Price | Coffee Production and Export (million bags) | Index of coffee Production | Index of Import Prices |
|------|------|------|------|------|------|
| 2001 | 11 | 78.6 | 6 | 83.3 | 90 |
| 2002 | 12 | 85.7 | 6.5 | 90.3 | 95 |
| 2003 | 14 | 100 | 7.2 | 100 | 100 |
| 2004 | 13 | 92.8 | 7.5 | 104.2 | 106 |
| 2005 | 18 | 128.6 | 6.2 | 86.1 | 110 |
| 2006 | 19 | 135.7 | 6.8 | 94.4 | 112 |
| 2007 | 22 | 157.1 | 7.3 | 101.3 | 110 |

b) The value of exports is the price per bag x the bags produced.

For 2001: $11 x 6m = $66m

For 2007: $22 x 7.3m = $160.6

c) To calculate the Terms of Trade (ToT) we divide the Index of export prices by the index of import prices and multiply by 100.

e.g. For 2001, ToT = (78.6/90) x 100 = 87.34

For 2002, ToT = (85.7/95) x 100 = 90.21 and so on.

d) With the exception of 2004 when the index fell from 100 to 87.5, the ToT has improved meaning that the index has increased.

e) If the value of imports in 2001 is $72m and from b) we know that the value of exports is $66m, then the value of net exports is $66m – $72m = – $6m.

f) If net exports are 3% of GDP, we can calculate GDP as ($6m/3) x 100 = $200m

## Question 17

a) The total revenue received by the Government = Tariff x imports = $20 x 1400 = $ 28000

b) Imports before the tariff = 3000 – 500 = 2500 and after the tariff = 2400 – 1000 = 1400 so reduction = 2500 – 1400 = 1100

c) The loss to world exporters is the reduction in imports (1100) x the pre tariff world price ($120) = 1100 x $120 = $132000

d) The loss of consumer surplus = the combined area 1+ 2+ 3+ 4.
Area 1+2+3 = 2400 x $20 = $48000 and the area of 4 is 600 x $20/2 = $6000 so the total loss is $48000 + $6000 = $54000

e) The deadweight loss = the area 2 + 4 = $5000 = $6000 = $11000

f) The % change in spending on steel = (change/original) x 100. Original = 3000 x $120 = $36000 New = 2400 x $140 = $336000

So % change = [($360000 – $336000)/$360000] x 100 = 6.67%

g) The increased cost to the car producer = Q x Tariff = 500 x $20 = $10000

## Question 18

a) Country A can produce more cars than B so it has AA in cars and B has AA in Wine.

b) Country A has the lowest opportunity cost for cars and B for Wine so A has CA in cars and B in Wine.

c) Comparative advantage shows a country where to specialize and gain from trade.

d) Total production if they specialize fully = 20 cars produced by A and 200 wine produced by B

e) Dividing resources between cars and wine means A produces 10 cars and 50 wine and B produces 5 cars and 100 wine so total = 15 cars and 150 wine.

f) Diagram

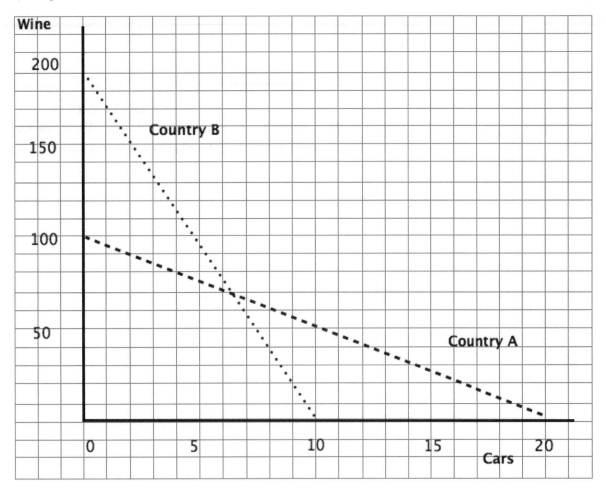

g) At the exchange rate 1car: 10wine, A gives up 2 cars and receives 20 wine. Domestically by giving up 2 cars A would receive 10 wine so it is better off by 10 wine. B gives up 20 wine and receives 2 cars. Domestically by giving up 20 wine it would receive 1 car so it is better off by 1 car.

# Part 2: Test Papers

1. A manufacturer of cotton trousers has the capacity to produce 60000 pairs of trousers per year, but currently produces 40000 pairs in total and sells them for €6 a pair. The manufacturer faces the following costs of production for the 40000 pairs of trousers annually.

| | |
|---|---|
| Rent for Premises | 10 000 |
| Advertising | 1 000 |
| Raw Materials | 15 000 |
| Direct Labour | 26 000 |
| Energy | 2 000 |
| Depreciation | 2 000 |
| Other Variable Costs | 2 000 |
| Other Fixed Costs Including Normal Profit | 10 000 |

a) Calculate the annual Fixed and Variable Costs of Production.          [2 marks]

................................................................................................................

................................................................................................................

................................................................................................................

b) Calculate Variable cost as a % of total cost.          [1 mark]

................................................................................................................

................................................................................................................

c) Calculate the annual supernormal profit. [3 marks]

.................................................................................................................
.................................................................................................................
.................................................................................................................

d) Define normal and supernormal profit. [2 + 2 marks]

.................................................................................................................
.................................................................................................................
.................................................................................................................
.................................................................................................................

e) If the firm receives an order for an additional 20000 pairs of trousers (bringing the total to 60000 pairs) for €1.20 a pair, should it accept the order (assuming it faces constant returns)? Explain your answer.

[4 marks]

.................................................................................................................
.................................................................................................................
.................................................................................................................
.................................................................................................................

f) Calculate the AVC for the additional 20000 pairs of trousers. [2 marks]

.................................................................................................................
.................................................................................................................
.................................................................................................................

g) Assuming that there are many competing firms in the market is this firm operating in perfect or monopolistic competition? Explain your answer. [4 marks]

.................................................................................................................
.................................................................................................................
.................................................................................................................
.................................................................................................................

h) Explain what will happen in this market in the long run. [5 marks]

.................................................................................................................
.................................................................................................................
.................................................................................................................
.................................................................................................................
.................................................................................................................
.................................................................................................................
.................................................................................................................
.................................................................................................................

2. The annual macroeconomic measurements for Atlantis and Pacifica are as follows:

| Country | Atlantis | Pacifica |
|---|---|---|
| GDP per capita ($ US) | 1000 | 1200 |
| Population (millions) | 5 | 8 |
| Adult Literacy (%) | 70 | 56 |
| Life Expectancy | 62 | 48 |

a) Calculate GDP in both countries. [2 marks]

.............................................................................................................................

.............................................................................................................................

.............................................................................................................................

b) Define the Human Development Index (HDI). [2marks]

.............................................................................................................................

.............................................................................................................................

.............................................................................................................................

c) With respect to the HDI which country is likely to have the higher ranking? Explain your answer. [4 marks]

.............................................................................................................................

.............................................................................................................................

.............................................................................................................................

.............................................................................................................................

.............................................................................................................................

.............................................................................................................................

d) Which country appears to have the better growth prospects? [2 marks]

.............................................................................................................................

.............................................................................................................................

.............................................................................................................................

.............................................................................................................................

e) Identify and explain three other factors that could influence living standards in these countries.                                                    [3 x 3 marks]

1.....................................................................................................................
.........................................................................................................................
.........................................................................................................................
.........................................................................................................................
.........................................................................................................................

2.....................................................................................................................
.........................................................................................................................
.........................................................................................................................
.........................................................................................................................
.........................................................................................................................

3.....................................................................................................................
.........................................................................................................................
.........................................................................................................................
.........................................................................................................................
.........................................................................................................................

If in Atlantis MPC = MPW and the full employment level of National Income (YF) = $6 Billion

f) Calculate the value of the multiplier.                                        [2 marks]

.........................................................................................................................
.........................................................................................................................

g) Calculate the increase in Government spending necessary to achieve YF.   [4 marks]

.........................................................................................................................
.........................................................................................................................
.........................................................................................................................
.........................................................................................................................
.........................................................................................................................

**3. The following table refers to Export and Import prices for Atlantis**

| Year | Index of Export Prices | Index of Import Prices |
|------|------------------------|------------------------|
| 2001 | 97 | 98 |
| 2002 | 100 | 100 |
| 2003 | 102 | 110 |
| 2004 | 105 | 112 |
| 2005 | 104 | 114 |
| 2006 | 106 | 120 |
| | | |

a) Define the Terms of Trade.                                              [2 marks]

......................................................................................................................
......................................................................................................................

b) Calculate the Terms of Trade for 2004 and 2005.                         [2 marks]

......................................................................................................................
......................................................................................................................
......................................................................................................................

c) Calculate the % change in import prices from 2003 to 2004.              [2 marks]

......................................................................................................................
......................................................................................................................

d) Describe the movement in the Terms of Trade index for the period 2004- 2006. [2 marks]

......................................................................................................................
......................................................................................................................
......................................................................................................................

e) Assuming that the demand for exports is elastic and the demand for imports is inelastic, estimate the effect of this movement in the Terms of Trade on the current account balance for Atlantis. [4 marks]

...........................................................................................................................
...........................................................................................................................
...........................................................................................................................
...........................................................................................................................
...........................................................................................................................

f) Given the effect on the current account identified in e), explain how this might affect the exchange rate of Atlantis' currency. [4 marks]

...........................................................................................................................
...........................................................................................................................
...........................................................................................................................
...........................................................................................................................
...........................................................................................................................

If Atlantis has a current account deficit of $200 million, an invisible trade surplus of $40 million, visible exports = $120 million and GDP = $5 billion

g) Calculate the visible trade balance. [2 marks]

...........................................................................................................................
...........................................................................................................................

h) Calculate the value of visible imports. [1 mark]

...........................................................................................................................

i) Calculate the trade balance as a % of GDP. [2 marks]

...........................................................................................................................
...........................................................................................................................

j) Identify and briefly explain one policy that Atlantis could implement to reduce its current account deficit. [4 marks]

...........................................................................................................................
...........................................................................................................................
...........................................................................................................................
...........................................................................................................................
...........................................................................................................................
...........................................................................................................................
...........................................................................................................................
...........................................................................................................................
...........................................................................................................................

**1. The only cinema in Bigtown has a total of 300 seats. It estimates the demand for tickets by adults to be as follows:**

| Price In $ | 15 | 14 | 13 | 12 | 11 | 10 | 9 | 8 | 7 | 6 | 5 | 4 | 3 | 2 | 1 |
|---|---|---|---|---|---|---|---|---|---|---|---|---|---|---|---|
| Quantity Demanded | 25 | 50 | 75 | 100 | 125 | 150 | 175 | 200 | 225 | 250 | 275 | 300 | 325 | 350 | 375 |

The total cost of showing any film = $900

a) Identify the market structure. [1 mark]

...........................................................................................................................

b) Calculate the profit maximizing ticket price. [4 marks]

...........................................................................................................................
...........................................................................................................................
...........................................................................................................................
...........................................................................................................................
...........................................................................................................................

c) Calculate the total profit. [2 marks]

...........................................................................................................................
...........................................................................................................................

d) Calculate the lowest price the cinema would charge to show a film. [2 marks]

...........................................................................................................................
...........................................................................................................................

e) Calculate the price that would maximize Total Revenue. [2 marks]

...........................................................................................................................
...........................................................................................................................

f) Comment on the marginal cost and price elasticity of demand at the revenue maximizing price. [4 marks]

...........................................................................................................................
...........................................................................................................................
...........................................................................................................................
...........................................................................................................................
...........................................................................................................................
...........................................................................................................................

**If in addition to the adult demand there was the following children's demand:**

| Price in $ | 5 | 4 | 3 | 2 | 1 |
|---|---|---|---|---|---|
| Quantity Demanded | 20 | 40 | 60 | 80 | 100 |

g)  Calculate how many children's tickets, in addition to the adult tickets, a profit maximizing cinema should sell and at what price. Explain your answer.                [4 marks]

.......................................................................................................................................
.......................................................................................................................................
.......................................................................................................................................
.......................................................................................................................................
.......................................................................................................................................
.......................................................................................................................................
.......................................................................................................................................

h) How would you describe the policy of charging different prices to different age groups and what are the conditions necessary for it to be practiced?                [4 marks]

.......................................................................................................................................
.......................................................................................................................................
.......................................................................................................................................
.......................................................................................................................................
.......................................................................................................................................
.......................................................................................................................................
.......................................................................................................................................

i) If the government imposed a 10% tax on adult tickets, how would this affect your answer to g)?                [2 marks]

.......................................................................................................................................
.......................................................................................................................................
.......................................................................................................................................
.......................................................................................................................................

2. The following table shows the taxes applied in two countries, A and B

| Annual Income In $ | Tax Rate in Country A (%) | Tax Rate in Country B (%) |
|---|---|---|
| 0 - 20000 | 0 | 10 |
| 20001- 40000 | 20 | 10 |
| 40000 + | 30 | 10 |

Country A applies a tax on all spending of 5%

Country B applies a tax on all spending of12%

a) Distinguish between direct and indirect taxes.                    [2 marks]

........................................................................................................

........................................................................................................

b) Define progressive, regressive and proportional tax systems.      [3 marks]

........................................................................................................

........................................................................................................

........................................................................................................

........................................................................................................

c) Describe the tax system in countries A and B.                   [4 marks]

........................................................................................................

........................................................................................................

........................................................................................................

........................................................................................................

........................................................................................................

**Tom, who lives in country A, has an annual income of $50000 and spends 60% of his disposable income.**

d) Calculate total amount of tax paid by Tom.                                    [4 marks]

........................................................................................................................
........................................................................................................................
........................................................................................................................
........................................................................................................................
........................................................................................................................
........................................................................................................................

e) Calculate the % of income Tom pays in income tax.                            [2 marks]

........................................................................................................................
........................................................................................................................

**If Tom moved to country B with no change in his income and spending**

f) Calculate the amount of tax paid by Tom and the % of his income paid in tax.

[4 marks]

........................................................................................................................
........................................................................................................................
........................................................................................................................
........................................................................................................................
........................................................................................................................

g) Explain which country is likely to have a larger Gini coefficient?           [3 marks]

........................................................................................................................
........................................................................................................................
........................................................................................................................
........................................................................................................................
........................................................................................................................

h) According to supply side economists like Laffer, which country is likely to have a greater disincentive to work and effort?                                    [3 marks]

........................................................................................................................
........................................................................................................................
........................................................................................................................
........................................................................................................................
........................................................................................................................
........................................................................................................................

**3. With a given quantity of resources country A can produce either 2 tractors or 4 cars and country B can produce either 4 tractors or 16 cars.**

a) Define the concepts of Absolute and Comparative Advantage.          [2 + 2 marks]

..................................................................................................................
..................................................................................................................
..................................................................................................................
..................................................................................................................

b) Identify the distribution of Absolute and Comparative Advantage between country A and B.          [2 marks]

..................................................................................................................
..................................................................................................................
..................................................................................................................

c) Calculate the opportunity cost of tractors in country A and B.          [2 marks]

..................................................................................................................
..................................................................................................................

d) At an exchange rate of 1 tractor for 3 cars show how both country A and country B would benefit from trade.          [4 marks]

..................................................................................................................
..................................................................................................................
..................................................................................................................
..................................................................................................................
..................................................................................................................

e) If a country wanted to reduce imports by a specific amount which form of protectionism should it apply? Explain your answer.          [3 marks]

..................................................................................................................
..................................................................................................................
..................................................................................................................
..................................................................................................................

f) Draw a clearly labeled diagram to show the PPC's for country A and B.     [4 marks]

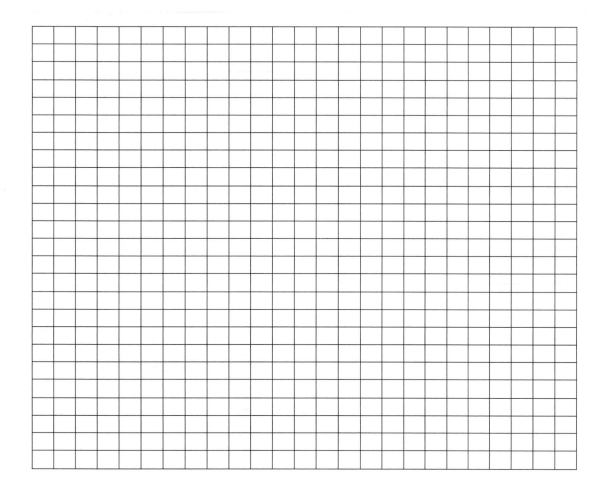

g) Identify and explain two additional benefits of specialization and trade.          [4 marks]

...................................................................................................................................
...................................................................................................................................
...................................................................................................................................
...................................................................................................................................
...................................................................................................................................

e) If country A improves its productivity in cars so that it can now produce either 2 tractors or 8 cars, how would this affect its trade with country B?          [2 marks]

...................................................................................................................................
...................................................................................................................................
...................................................................................................................................
...................................................................................................................................

### Paper 1

### Question 1

a) FC = Rent $10000 + Advertising $1000 + Depreciation $2000 + Other $10000 = $23000
VC = Materials $15000 + Direct Labour $26000 + Energy $2000 + Other $2000 = $45000.

b) TC = FC + VC = $23000 + $45000 = $68000. VC as % = (VC/TC) x 100

 = (45000/68000) x 100 = 66.1%

c) TR = P x Q = $6 x 40000 = $240000, TC = $68000, Profit = TR – TC

= $240000 – $ 68000 = $172000

d) Normal profit is the minimum amount necessary to keep the firm in business, it is the opportunity cost of the entrepreneur and is achieved when TC = TR.

Supernormal profit is any amount in excess of normal profit and is achieved when TR>TC.

e) New order would provide additional revenue of 20000 x $1.20 = $24000. Since we have excess capacity and constant returns, the additional cost for 20000 will be half the VC for 40000, that is  $22500, so order will increase profit by: $24000 – $22500 = $1500.

f) AVC = TVC/Q = 22500/20000 = $1.12

g) The main difference between perfect and monopolistic competition is the nature of the product. In perfect competition it is homogeneous, but in monopolistic competition it is differentiated. Since the firm engages in advertising it means that products are differentiated and therefore the market structure must be monopolistic competition.

h) A feature of both perfect and monopolistic competition is perfect freedom of entry and exit; therefore since the firm is earning supernormal profit, new firms will be attracted to enter the industry. As these firms enter, the demand faced by existing firms will decrease and the process will continue until all firms are earning normal profit and the market will be in long run equilibrium.

### Question 2

a) GDP = GDP per capita x population. For Atlantis GDP = $1000 x 5million = $5billion, for Pacifica, GDP = $1200 x 8million = $9.6billion

b) HDI is a composite index which aims to measure economic and social welfare by including income, education and health care indicators.

c) Pacifica has a higher income per head, but Atlantis has a higher life expectancy and adult literacy, so overall it is likely that Atlantis has a higher HDI than Pacifica.

d) Atlantis is likely to have better growth prospects because its superior health and education will increase labour productivity thus increasing its potential output.

e)      1. Income distribution: the more unequal this is, the less representative the per capita income figure.

      2. Relative prices: For better accuracy the $ value of GDP should be calculated at PPP rather than market exchange rates.

      3. Parallel economy: this refers to unrecorded economic activity which varies between countries. The larger it is the less accurate the official GDP figures.

f) Since MPC + MPW = 1, and MPC = MPW, then MPW = 0.5. The multiplier (K) = 1/MPW

= 1/0.5 = 2

g) Since Y = GDP = $5bn, and YF = $6bn, Income must increase by $1bn. K = 2 so the increase in Government spending necessary to close the gap is $1bn/2 = $0.5bn

*Question 3*

a) ToT = (Index of Export prices/Index of Import Prices) x 100

b) ToT 2004 = (105/112) x 100 = 93.7, 2005 = (104/114) x100 = 91.2

c) The % change in import prices = (change in price/original price) x 100 = 2/110 x 100 = 1.8%

d) ToT 2006 = (106/120) x 100 = 88.3, so from 2004 to 2006 the ToT has deteriorated.

e) Since import prices have increased significantly and demand is inelastic, the spending on imports will increase and lead the current account towards deficit

f) Ceteris paribus, and increased deficit will cause the exchange rate to depreciate

g) Current account = Visible + Invisible trade = – $200 – $40 = – $240m

h) Visible deficit = X – M = –$240m,since X = $120m, M = $360m

i) Trade balance as % GDP = (240m/5bn) x 100 = 4.8%

j) Policies to reduce deficit are either expenditure reducing or expenditure switching e.g. a depreciation of the currency to make exports more competitive relative to imports thus switching expenditure to domestic products.

## Question 1

a) Monopoly because it is the only cinema.

b) Since cost is the same regardless of tickets sold ($900) the profit maximizing price will be where TR is highest. Highest TR occurs when ticket price + $8, since $8 x 200 tickets = $1600, and no other TR is higher.

c) Profit = TR – TC = $1600 – $900 = $700.

d) Lowest price is $4 because at this price the maximum number of seats is filled (300).

e) Same as b).

f) TR is maximized where MR = 0 and where demand is of unit elasticity.

g) Calculating TR for each price we find that price $3 and 60 tickets is best (TR = $180).

h) This is described as price discrimination which is the sale of the same product at different prices to different groups of consumers. The conditions necessary are: monopoly power, no possibility of resale and different elasticity of demand in each separated market.

i) There will be no change because MC and MR are unaffected.

## Question 2

a) Direct taxes are taxes on incomes whereas indirect taxes are taxes on expenditure.

b) Progressive: where % of income paid in tax increases with income, regressive: where % of income paid in tax decreases with income and proportional: where % of income paid in tax remains the same as income changes.

c) A has a progressive tax system because income tax rates increase with income and regressive indirect tax is low. B has a proportional income tax but a higher indirect tax so overall the system is regressive.

d) Tom will pay no tax on the first $20000, 20% on the next $20000 and 30% on $10000, so Tom's tax = 0 + $4000 + $3000 = $7000. His disposable income (Yd) is $50000 – $7000 = $43000. He spends 60% of Yd i.e. $43000 x (60/100) = $25800 and pays 5% in tax i.e. $25800 x (5/100) = $1290. Total tax paid = $7000 + $1290 = $8290.

e) % income in income tax = (tax/income) x 100 = (7000/50000) x 100 = 14%

f) Income tax is now 10% on all income i.e. $50000 x 10% = $5000.

Yd = $50000 – $5000 = $45000. 60% Yd is spent i.e. $45000 x 60% = $27000 and this is taxed at 12% i.e. $27000 x 12/100 = $3240.

Total tax paid is $5000 + $3240 = $8240. As a % of income this is
(8240/50000) x 100 = 16.5%

g) B because tax system is regressive so income will be less equally distributed.

h) A because of the progressive income tax system which might have a disincentive effect.

*Question 3*

a)  Absolute Advantage (AA): country can produce more with a given quantity of factors, Comparative Advantage (CA): country can produce a product at a lower opportunity cost.

b) Country B has AA in both and CA in cars, country A has CA in tractors.

c) Opportunity cost ratio in A is 1 tractor: 2 cars and in B 1 tractor: 4 cars.

d) With an exchange rate of 1tractor for 3 cars both countries will benefit. Country A will receive 3 cars in exchange for 1 tractor. Domestically it would only gain 2 cars for 1 tractor so it gains 1 car. Country B would have to give up 4 cars domestically for 1 tractor, but now receives 1 tractor for 3 cars so it also gains 1 car.

e) A quota would be best because it is the only measure which specifies a quantity restriction.

f) Diagram

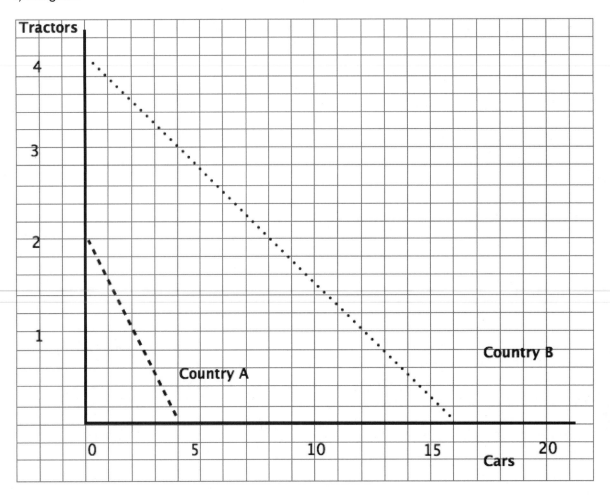

g) Specialisation may lead to scope for economies of scale and the development of expertise in production through "learning by doing".

h) There will be no gains from trade because they will now have the same opportunity cost ratios.